A GASH IN THE DARKNESS

A GASH IN THE DARKNESS

CHRISTOPHER SOUTHGATE

Printed by imprintdigital
Upton Pyne, Exeter
www.imprintdigital.net

Typeset by narrator
www.narrator.me.uk
enquiries@ narrator.me.uk

Published by Shoestring Press
19 Devonshire Avenue, Beeston, Nottingham, NG9 1BS
(0115) 925 1827
www.shoestringpress.co.uk

First published 2012

ISBN 978 1 907356 48 3

ACKNOWLEDGEMENTS

I thank the Nida Institute for Biblical Scholarship at the American Bible Society for their commission of the poem 'Rendering Voices', which formed part of the launch of the 2011 International Meeting of the Society of Biblical Literature.

Some of these poems were published in the chapbook *Incident Light* (Eyelet Books, 2009).

'In My Black Hat' was commended in the 2009 National Poetry Competition.

'Île St Louis' first appeared in *Easing the Gravity Field* (Shoestring Press, 2006)

Versions of some of these poems appeared first in the following magazines: *Ars Interpres, Otter, Outposts,* and *Temenos Academy Review.*

As ever I thank my editor John Lucas for his friendship and sustained encouragement, as well as his always constructive feedback. I am also very grateful for the discerning critical responses of Julie-Ann Rowell, Hilary Menos, Candy Neubert and Richard Skinner to drafts of these poems.

CONTENTS

For my wife Sandy
in deep gratitude for our thirty years of marriage

I. Will It Stop When One Wants to Be Quiet?

Will it stop when one wants to be quiet?
O tell me the truth about love.
– *W.H. Auden*

BIRDS

A blonde, perched across the back of a bike
while her man pedals.
She sends a text that makes her laugh,
gives her lover's ribs a squeeze,
doffs her hat to a traffic cop.
They speed down off a bridge,
like free bloody birds, as Larkin said.

How many of those exhilarate moments
in our love
could anyone have seen?

Only we in the world
that day in Amsterdam
when sunlight filled a room lined with mirrors
watched reflections of watered light
dance on a gilded ceiling,
shimmer, weave and interweave, twine, beat on each other, beat...

A bright day
edged by gables.
A secret taking flight.

LEAVING

From the window he watched her
for the last time.

He knew he would always remember
the curve of her body in the sunlight.

He half told himself
he would somehow be back
knowing it was not true.

He knew he would always remember
that old, wise expression that would sometimes come over her
face.

He realised there'd been others.
That he could never explain to anyone
what it meant to be with her.

He knew he would always remember
how she made him look at stars.

If he was honest,
she could be a chill friend,
so stern in her loveliness.

But he knew he would always remember
how she made him feel about his life, his home.

If he was honest,
he missed playfulness in her,
fresh rain, shaken out of branches by sudden breeze.

He knew deeper mysteries were denied him.
He breathed the wrong air, would always move in the wrong circles.

From the window he watched her
for the last time.

Eugene A. Cernan, USN, Apollo 17.

TOWER

My first love lived at the top of a tower.
My rival and I once passed on her stair.
Each telling of this story alters its colour,
Dulling my sense of hating him then.

My rival and I once passed on her stair –
He in a sort of sadness I had never seen,
Dulling my sense of hating him then –
I in ascending, baffled shyness

He in a sort of sadness I had never seen
Of love without sex, sex without love,
I in ascending baffled shyness
Not quite believing in myself, or her.

Love without sex, sex without love,
I learned both things in that blurred time,
Not quite believing in myself, or her.
Living by moments, filling empty memory –

I learned both things in that blurred time.
Each telling of this story alters its colour –
Living by moments, filling empty memory
With how my love lived at the top of a tower.

HUMMINGBIRDS

A hummingbird is like a fencer,
At each bloom perfectly intent,
Offering in *sixte*, seeing the opening
To lunge his beak in *quarte*
And escape, all energy, free

Until his proud parabolic
Zooming in and out of pinetrunks
Is cut by another's, a rival dive,
Pull-out, turn, jink, attack,
Beating away chivalry.

Then the rival courts the flowers,
Presentation neat, poise delicate,
Each thrust when it comes
Quickness, each break
Full of forgetfulness.

I had done this. We had all done it.
Crickets sang. Cicadas jam-sessioned
Random laughter. You were my
Trumpet-flower, bright and full
Of your own light

You were my new moon, splintered
By all these contests among the pines.
Now our loving, much a blur,
Hovers sometimes motionless, gathering
Quanta, feeding on improbability.
We can watch the birds, and sigh,
And laugh, and watch the age fall.

TWO MEMORIES

Driving down Glen Isla, first girlfriend
Alongside, sex to come and our favourite Tokay
And laughing at nothing. A strange new language
Rapidly learned. After all this time
I cannot remember her voice. Only how
Aloneness, and longing, and having
To pretend, were briefly set to rest.
A moment of emptiness, yet lacking
All tristesse.

Walking through Piazza San Marco
On a cold morning early. Workmen
Unpacking crates. The night's rain
Streaming into the canal. The old
Doomed basilica huddled
Magnificent in its space.
Perhaps
We shall never see Venice again
But here we had sat in a house where Turner lived,
And Proust, talking for an hour about a statue of a boy,
And emerged to a single moment of flamboyant Turner light
Over an unknown palace.

THE PHOTOGRAPHS AT THE MARRIAGE OF AN OLD FRIEND

are on a powerpoint loop
between the reception and the ceilidh.
Many mountainsides and toboggans,
friends and interiors.
Twenty years of mood pictures -
man reading, woman digging,
kids cooking.

Before them the student snaps.
How earnestly sure of life
are those faces. How we thought we knew
each other, and were grown up,
and belonged, without compromise.

Occasionally it was strawberry time in the Parks.
More often it was dark, and bent bicycles,
cold, and two hundredth in the queue for Upper Hall.
It was picking our way along an unfamiliar ridge
falling often into a huge scoured corrie of missed chances.
It was a blaze of eyes, a puzzle-cube of hearts - I solve it only now
from a powerpoint loop of strangers.

RETURN TO THE ROYAL SOCIETY

Twenty-one. Convinced my questions
are all worth asking.
Tackled the speaker
on intercalation into DNA
and rejected his answer
as inadequate.

My hair is long -
my father hates it.
He has given up on
my academic potential
as I should give up
on the girl in the next lab.
But in truth I remember my day at the Royal
for her delicious, half-mocking smile
when I asked my pushy question.

Fifty-something. Beginning to look
disturbingly like my father.
No less opinionated, but less desperate for attention.
Before the session I read
the latest Heaney - some of it I can definitely learn from -
and plan my classes for the term after next.

I am dissatisfied with the speakers
on stem cell technology.
But at least I know now how hard they've worked -
how tough it is to make an impact,
build a structure that convinces.
I file away nuances of the Zeitgeist,
escape mercifully unnoticed,
remember my second day at the Royal
for the faint smile on the portrait of Christopher Wren.

HIS MEMORIES OF HER ARE ALL OF THE DECEITFULNESS OF SUNLIGHT

his whole life filled up with discarded sunlight
days wasted on misreadings of her eyes.

There was a day given grace by desperate sunlight
by one's need and another's longing.

She told him of pain, walking hard in the charged sunlight.
and he listened, glowing with it.

He showed her gingko leaves, spiralling down the light
like the sheen of sun on lemonskin,
cutting the brightness,
and how one had lodged perfectly in a magnolia branch.

That was the day she told him she loved him
her words lying down
in the unseen sunlight.

CHLORIDES AND TRIALS

Michael Faraday admitted to his future wife that she must vie for his affections with 'chlorides and trials, oil, Davy, steel, miscellanies, mercury and fifty other professional fancies'.

You should have been warned
that first time we got up at three a.m.
to change the tubes
on my chromatography column.

You should have thought better of it
when I said listening to harpsichord music
in the lab was romantic
like you holding my legs
as I changed the chloride level
in the topmost elution chamber.

There should have been danger signs
in the mounting piles of books
on the Cappadocian Fathers
Pseudo-Dionysius by the fireside.

Because you did not heed the warnings
we have talked mercury toxicity,
'Steel Magnolias', and Donald Davie,
and fifty cadences of childhood.
Because of your stubbornness
in vying for my attention

every snowfall still drags us
stiffly out from our chairs
hunting out gloves, hats,
toboggan, candle-wax,
forging off in search of
the ideal friction-compensated slope.

SMOKE

Larches in the last light.
Toast burned while we snatch a kiss.
Lapsang Souchong tea.

ORCHARD

What is remembered in this orchard? Laughter
like a conspiracy of birds. Being young,
leaning against a cherry tree. A song
starting. Kisses, promises, ever after.
This was the light, the music of our early
loving. Or such is my account of it.
Your version has my damp but handy bed-sit
colluding with our lonely hungry folly.

I go back to the orchard. Cherry trees
lichened, cankered. A brief drift
of white and pink – the blossom's random gift.
I hear again the song, your words, my pleas.
I see the weightless loveliness of truth.
I see each petal hurl itself to earth.

II. In My Black Hat

IN MY BLACK HAT

Thora Dardel sees her portrait by Modigliani for the first time in forty-six years.

I am not the woman you see sitting in the corner
at the private view. My name is Dardel.
In nineteen nineteen, in Montparnasse,
I was painted by the dying Modigliani.
He sketched me in a café. He devoured me
with his eyes. He took me
to Rue de la Grande-Chaumiére, number eight.

I see you hesitate. Yes, how faded I have become.
You ask whether he was good to be with, this Amedeo?
Ah no. He drank continually, and spat blood,
and still if Jeanne had not been there, and the child,
he would have consumed me.

I could see her in a small painting behind his head –
a long oval face with almond eyes,
heart-stopping, lovely, cursed eyes
that cursed you as you looked at them.
The flat smelled of coal dust.
As you see I wore my black hat
and kept my hands in my lap.

I have lived in Paris, and Stockholm,
and Montevideo. I have family who love me.
But tonight at last it is clear.
I am not the woman you see sitting in the corner
stiffly, slow-speaking, preferring her own company.

I am that young student,
in thrall to a dying painter,
in love with Nils Dardel,
sitting in my black hat
with my head on one side

and I always shall be.

DIMENSIONS

A world of verticals. Sunlight paints
The higher spires, lifts the whole Gothic cosmos
Up to the glow of heaven.
Weight is buttressed elsewhere. Glass
Floods inner space with a stain of colour
Some call joy.

Dark hulls sidle towards
A shadowed entrance. They bring petty introductions
From many forgotten princes.
The grand salon emits a faint, violet
Light, smells sweetly
Of over-sprayed silk.

On a sharp black table, a single espresso
Entitled The Impossibility of Knowledge.
A whole industry of deferred theory
Exults and squabbles.

PHOTOGRAPHING RODIN'S EVE - AN EXHIBITION

Early work used gum bichromate,
recovered little light, picked out
only the gleam on bronze shoulders
hugged away from the world.
Now in the high lissom sunlight
at Kettle's Yard we can see
Iraida Icaza, 2006.
Gelatin silver and selenium
split tone prints on fibre paper.
She wraps Eve in translucent
plastic wrapping, she has the bronze
turned, keeps the camera still.
Eve spins slowly out of focus,
always hiding her face.

I remember my gum bichromate days -
in the dark about life, my only tone
the overexposed gleam of being young
with its hugged-shouldered shames.
I have had years of training
(starting at Kettle's Yard)
in trying to keep the camera still.
I remember the yellow-gold glory
of an unrepeatable moon.
I am being laid down (while I try
to wrap myself in film, I turn and turn)
into the fibre of the world.
Whatever is silver in the gift of my life
spins slowly towards paradise.

ON NOT BEING MISTAKEN FOR JOHNNY DEPP

Invited to give a weighty address.
At dinner beforehand, a chance to assess
the audience. They look over-keen,
feisty; I fear some of them mean
to take me down a peg or two.

The tech person, Hungarian, twenty
(at most), dresses me in mikes, with plenty
of phono-lead, rope to hang myself on.
She looks me up and down,
grins, says I'll do.

I think of a problem, apologise. 'Hard
to please,' I say, 'these lecturers, like film stars.'
She agrees, adjusts my gear,
considers me again, adds in my ear,
'but not handsome'.

So I am destroyed, in the end,
not by the crabbed college expert or his friend,
the ones who knew far more than I
about the Quattrocento in Italy –
not a tantrum

out of them, they were pussycats, the best –
but by the girl from Buda, or more likely Pest,
who failed to see the raffish subversive arresting heart-throb
I am within. Mistook me for just another job –
more middle-aged anxiety.

My revenge is calculated, bold,
savage, and served cold.
After deep and careful thought
I decide that I will boycott
Pirates of the Caribbean III.

CONISTON, WINTER

Fog-films, faintly luminous,
graze the marshes.

In the fields, meltpools,
pale steel discs of mirrored sky.

On the massif, hanging cloud
softens the ice-scars.

Slabs of slate by the shore
smudged with the charcoal of long-ago lichens.

The ribbon of the lake
this windless morning

is the Platonic form of grayness
swallowing the colours of the woods,

transmuting day into waterlight
thinking its way
                    out to infinity.

THE CROIX DE GUERRE, ET CETERA

The day before we leave for Paris,
I write up the record of the trip.

"The sun shone. We walked late
in a warm breeze, café-surfing.
The Musée d'Orsay transformed our view
of van Gogh. By Notre Dame
we talked with an old, old man
wearing the *Croix de Guerre*
and driving a horse-cart. Behind him
the flying buttresses soared weightless, et cetera, et cetera."

The next day a fatality
on the line to the Tunnel –
someone with a name like Sonia, or Colin,
someone with a label like depressive,
or untreatable –
makes for a delay – grimy, crowded,
stranding us in English sandwich-bars.

And we prove not to have quite the edge or energy
of ten years ago, when we walked
the whole Left Bank at midnight,
stopping only for onion soup.
Nor are we sure how it will be between us
when we are alone so much together, et cetera, et cetera.

Paris, they say, is a moveable feast.
But now we need it
to stay still for us.
To be, *tout simple*, its light, its air,
its long avenues like flung ribbons of summer.
And it is. It is.

ÎLE ST LOUIS

A man in the best leather sandals
And a sensible scarf
Inches his way along the parapet
Of the Quai de Bourbon.

He turns at the first birch tree now
The breeze from the west
Is keener than it was.

The pile of unopened bills
On the Second Empire secretaire
Grows higher. His income is the interest
On moments:
                    The day the sentries of the *Waffen-SS*
Left the Pont Louis-Philippe for ever;
The day Marie brought him cherry blossom;
Dinner when he talked with Sartre.

The year before he turned at the Pont Neuf
Last year at the second tree.
This year the first.
By these markers he sees time pass.

He turns, still talking with Sartre,
The waiter at the corner café makes him a small bow.
The woman who spoke to him
At the service for Marie, considers him,
And turns right with her terrier, across the bridge.

By these gifts, and the steep grey faces
Of the Hotel de Ville, by the remembered
Sheets of colour at the Sainte Chapelle,
Where he used to pray when no-one was praying,
And the expressionless river,
And a weekly phone call from his daughter at Yale
He receives his days.

YALE

The train gets to New Haven at seven.
A cab to Starbucks, a hazelnut mocha
before I hit the Beinecke. My slob-out time
resisting the exactness of the archive.
I read *Le Figaro* and the TLS.
Sometimes I write to my father. Letters
link me in to the rhythm of his life -
how he survives, deep inside himself.

It is later in the day that I think of my mother.
I have lunch with some man, wonder
how she would have handled him.
I have a few things of hers - the *Légion d'Honneur*
from her work with the *Maquis*, a painting I once gave her
of leopards.

People say I live in Starbucks and the Beinecke
that my life is franchised to the care of the letters of the great.
That is the edge of me. The rest is in Paris -
there I am the keeper of the secrets of my mother's deathbed -
the concealments, the courage, the slammed doors
of arbitrary arrest. The release of someone other.

I love without hope the man who once taught me Beckett.
Our walk in the Luxembourg has the utter rightness of dream,
is a film tolerant of an infinite number of rewinds.
I sit at the tip of the Ile de la Cité
swinging my legs over the river where it parts.
My father tells me to draw back; my mother laughs.
I walk all the way from the Pont Neuf to the Etoile
singing, and I never once complain.

The train gets to New Haven at seven.

A RHYTHM OF DAYS - GREENWICH VILLAGE, AUTUMN

I tell myself all sorts of lies
on days like these, about love
and fame and beauty.

Staying within a thumbnail of the city

feeling the whole world stream past me
warm breeze intoxicant through my skin
grime and slush held at bay,

walking over to Sixth to the same diner for lunch,
down Macdougal every evening
for the same gelato, jazz at Blue Note,

sitting by the fountain in the Square
where the breeze slides the water jets
across each other, across rainbows,

scatters the notes of the skiffle band
among the surrounding sirens,
rearranges the trees' gift of their summer's life.

I tell myself all sorts of true things
on days like these, about rainbows
and saxophones, and the skid of bone-dry leaves.

TORCELLO

They like bricks here.
The path from the vaporetto is herringboned brick.
You walk this neat pilgrim way
As far as the basilica, which raises plain brick walls
Straight up toward heaven.
You may escape here with your learning and your current gospel:
The walls, unadorned, aloof on their columns
Tell you this is all straw.

The bishop of the place was elevated, via steep brick steps
So he might stare the better
At the stark laddered crucifix
                    And beyond it, the Last Judgment.
Only the Virgin, vast in black on a pale gold ground,
Contemplates this vision with serenity.
The walls tell you: sit quiet – in the humblest place –
Until you feel the Judgment is behind you.

ST GUILHEM-LE-DÉSERT, CLOISTER

On the hills above
ruined towers of hermits.

In a small rectangular pool
a few carp.

A simple garden
given over to herbs.

At the lavender flowers, a butterfly, then two
negotiate the hot breeze.

Cricket-song serrates
thousand-year-old quiet.

MONTPELLIER

Taking a place in
is all a matter of tempo.
Only on the fourth morning
am I slow enough to notice
the cedar doors of that foursquare palace,
its delicate balconies,
the leaning of that plane tree
in a gentle curve
towards the winter sun.

Give me a week
and I shall start to hear
the Cathedral bell chime the quarters,
smell the bread that old painter collects every morning,
savour the exaggerated pains
with which that young mother
adjusts the canopy of the pushchair
as she wheels her new baby
into the day's brightness.

Give me a month
and I shall know the winds
of Montpellier:
the one from the Sahara
hot on the skin;
the one off the Massif Central;
the wind from the sea where Shelley died.
Give me two months
and I shall know the winds by name.

Give me a year here
and I might start to see
who I have become.

CATHÉDRALE ST PIERRE, MONTPELLIER

The limbs of oaks make an intricate lattice
through which cathedral towers shine.
A blackbird sings an Occitanic blackbird song.
The towers lean their weight
on two massive cylinders of stone,
float above them, sentinel,
playing with the evening sunlight.
Their task is to praise
to be admired
to strike the hours to eternity.
They leave the hard geometry to the trees.

ARRIVING IN VENICE BY NIGHT

Across distances of oily water,
anonymous, lightless. Finally
a gathering of palaces
like film-sets stored in rows.

Thrown out at the Rialto,
left to pick our way
past surges of wanderers
we escape into streets a yard wide.

Above a small tenth-century door
a Byzantine mosaic of the Madonna in prayer.
Two lamps are lit nightly
fulfilling a sea-captain's promise.

A place of thousand-year-old vows
and plunder from every century.

We lose our way in a succession of alleys
that all lead back to a dark square
smelling of mediaeval brawls, petty treacheries,
poniards in the ribs.

A tower
whispers of seclusion, suicide.
We turn a corner, read a burnished plate
on an ancient door. Wake Forest University, it proclaims.

The old, doomed city
re-sold into the far distance.

TWO SURVIVORS

In Amsterdam the synagogue
for Sephardi. How did this
dark sanctuary of jacaranda wood
escape the Nazi pick-axe?
What story does that tell
of bribery, unknown love,
administrative omission?
Of a ravaged community
and five years daily expecting
final desecration.
I am required to keep my hat on
to pray, to wonder,
to give thanks.

In Istanbul the ancient church
of the Holy Peace. Massive walls
draw the eye up to a simple hollow cross.
How did this plainness
escape the iconists? What whim of the Sultan
left this one church
a storehouse not a mosque?
The great walls might still
be holding their breath,
awaiting the next twist of history.
I have no sense of that, only of their
strong serene vocation
to hold a space hollow with glory.

IRANIAN MINIATURES

A red diamond

At the limits of sight
as at the deepest turn of the deepest canyon
a colour from a place
of extreme yet generous force.
A colour only at home in this world
on the dying Dido's throat.

Golden Bowl

A good emerald set into the base
draws the eye not to the stone
but to the way echoing colour
stains the metal's depths
makes of gold
more than itself.

Mould-blown glass from Neishabur

Bursts of smoke and gold
the green of many different seas
and veins of darkness.

Women at the conference

Chamron-clad, moving
like short-stepping black birds,
composed within themselves,
full of unreadable thoughts.

And a young girl

No more than eight
just too young for the *hijab*
her chestnut curls
light up the Summit Hall.

MAUNA ULU, HAWAII

A good volcano invigorates the day
(while I still have my health,
select my sunlight, my vantage-points).
I watch the column of acid spray
flex like a curtain on the whim
of a thousand-mile ocean breeze.
Steam plays
against high, racing cloud.
I collect a piece of wood,
new-petrified, its crystalline gray
will set off the fig-tree
in my window.

Night. Same long slope, rainforest, lava-tarmac;
different regime, different law.
A random reddish glow across the hill,
scattered smoke from open wounds,
the forest-edge at war
with a million infiltrations of orcs.
Their camp-fires breed
dull dissonant light from the maw
of the world. Mauna Ulu
proliferates from within.

From where I stand, the triage zone,
I suddenly see the condition terminal –
this planet's lovely, green, breathing skin
a glorious, doomed cloaking
of ash and bone.

THE FOURTH PLINTH

The Fourth Plinth programme, now the responsibility of the Mayor of London, commissions various works to fill the vacant plinth in Trafalgar Square.

The current competitors are a six-storey windmill,
five mirrors,
four meerkhats,
a three-masted ship in a bottle,
a burned-out car (two-door)
and an empty space protected by a net.

I claim all four plinths
for what I would want always to remember.

On the first I place
the thorn-crowned man,
a young Jewish kingdom-prophet.
London dwarfs him. He
eclipses it.

On the second two holograms
of your face as we wake –
one to hold your loveliness,
one to track the surprise across your eyes
as you remember
how hard and long we have loved.

On the third I place
my three best teachers –
a scientist, a priest and a poet,
absolute in their integrity, their lives
asymptotic to compromise.

The fourth is harder, I concede.
I place on it
the light on the Wallabrook, the breeze off Hawaii,
and the Skye wind beating up out of Cor'Uisg.
My last talk with my mother.
Scraps of the Times Crossword, uncompleted.
Nudes by Titian and Modigliani,
surge of Beethoven seven,
the high Sierra from Half-Dome,
and a mating combination
for knights at chess.

I reserve the right to change this provision at sunset.
I bring in how the lead lights rattled
in my grandmother's door as it opened,
how a leopard moves through long grass,
my son driving the green at the fourteenth,
and the whole Appalachian Trail, in fall colour.

To save space, and in the interests of economy,
the whole of Bach, Plato and TS Eliot
are available on an IPod,
neatly placed between the transeptal towers
of Exeter Cathedral.

There are some more private moments.
I show these in the darkness
with Trafalgar Square cordoned off
and the lions hooded, for modesty.
The actors know their parts.
We dance them without rehearsal or regret.

Only my request for the whole city of Venice
on a fine sharp day in winter
has caused the Mayor concern.
Health and Safety are afraid I may take a chill, and sue,
and so bump up the congestion charge.

III. For Ben, and Karen, and others

COMING TO TERMS

Where are these terms
they are telling me
I must come to?

What they are saying to me
is that I am not as they are
(they thank their God)

But I could be - will be -
when I have come -
as they put it - to terms.

I nod my head
I do not say
(for this would make them uncomfortable)

that terms is a place
I do not want to come to
for that would be to say

that you are gone
that this colour of sky
the streets at evening

empty, endlessly walked,
this sound of dawn
this scent of waking alone

are the real colours, sounds,
scents of things,
without you there.

That my dream
in which you lie by my side

and tell me again of your love
and kiss my heart better
is a dream.

Terms is a place
of present tenses
laboriously corrected to past.

It is down a long tunnel –
once in there I might lose sight
of the lines of your face.

Coming to terms would mean accepting
that others have felt this before
and will again,

that these conversations
in which I tell you everything
are only one-way.

Terms might even be a place
where I had parted with your clothes
packed up your books, your music.

Terms is a far-off country.
It lies beyond
many stilted storytellings.

I do not choose
to come there.

BLUE MOON, NEW YEAR'S EVE, 2009

The thirteenth full moon of the year.

A young man,
whose mother is dying,
holds aloft the last candle lantern.
It lurches into the air, swings,
snags on a high branch.

The last pink berry
on the Himalayan rowan.
How the lantern shook itself into the night air
and rose into the aureole of the moon.
Sharp sound of frosted leaves under boots.

The lantern
lost to sight
driven by a keen wind from the north.
The full-hearted hug of a friend
outliving her dying.

DREWSTEIGNTON CHURCHYARD, FROM THE EAST

An arc of gravestones across a ridge.
They are prehistoric in this gloom.
Bars of cloud the colour of smoke
pale, fade to a charcoal blur.

A crow mobs a hungry raptor
which flips up its talons
before straggling off
in search of new rabbit vantage.

On the trees lichens lose the last of their colour,
branches sharpen to Indian inks
and a film of mist sidles eastwards
hugging the ice-hard ground.

Exactly one star awaits the moonrise.

In the arc of my life
this is a time of exact gladness
at the drain of light
out of a loved place.

A time for fighting for points of last vantage,
of recognising a fierce affection
for the ground that will claim
my worn-out body.

A stone will be thrown up
which a future student of twilight's inks
will read only as part of the curve
of a loved ridge.

HE WENT OUT TO A DESERTED PLACE

Deserted by love – familiar enough.
Love comes always erratically
to her assignations.

Deserted by goodness.
That is to have old suspicions confirmed.

Deserted by meaning. That
is the lifeless shelf of sand
surrounded by ocean, the dark thicket,
the address where even Job's God
is not at home, and prayer
disappears without trace. Once you find this place
it proves to be everywhere.

I.T.U.

The lived-out minutes, ground out into hours.
Intensive Care's neutral, functional seating.
Carrier-bags and travel-mugs.
Erratic drip-feed of information.
Clotting in the ventricles, cycles of sedation,
Cranial pressure, periods of hope.

You tell of touching his hand,
Your eyes dry, beyond the tears
That fell as early alleluias,
Tell that when even touching and talking
Were forbidden
Love carried, carried.

'STORMY WEATHER', 1995-2010

As the euthanizing pentabarbitone takes hold
My wife strokes our old cat's paws.

I lay an old white pillowcase on the body.
It would be hard to find the words for why.

I wind up our clock, aggressively,
Asserting order. The face-plate is of brass.

It will outlast the flimsy armour of our flesh,
Whatever tears are shed over our love.

The next day I check the time, head for the car,
Engage electronic climate control,

And call up Mozart. I talk through dry tears
To all those I have ever lost.

I think about moor-light, and a ring of silver birches.
It would be hard to find the words for why.

CHEMOTHERAPY

I.

A world of rules and sequences.
Day one, day eight, rest.
Methotrexate, folinate, rest.

Poisons and antidotes succeed each other
in tone-rows lacking all harmony.
Garish chords of optimism

clash horribly, use up our time.

II.

I nurse, as best I can,
the you that is – or may be –
growing cells which would change everything.

Sometimes your song is the same
as the sunlight in the woods
where we first loved.

Sometimes you tell me
we're worlds apart.
I cannot grow your cells

or feel your sudden hatred
for the Monet on the wall
or the smell of strawberries.

So the words I say at those times
are always lies,
spoken to the set of cells

I choose to guess you are.

III.

Our house assumes the cast
of a house of old age.
Pill bottles
line the windowsill.

There is more of your hair
left in the bath
than either of us
cares to mention.

There is the bluish haze
of winter light
on Devon trees.

ASHES

Scorhill Down, Dartmoor

His headed rapidly earthwards.
All his rhetoric, bombast,
had been thundered out –
all his courage spent.
What was left of his struggle
lacked affinity with Ariel's spells
sought the security of the granite pluton.

Hers hung on the wind
like fine sunlit rain
as though taking a last look
at the loved sweep of the moor
poised with strict gladness
between earth and heaven.
A decorous, seemly leave-taking.

Eight of us, the ones left,
stumble off the Down,
hearts beating briefly together,
soon enough scattered.

IN MEMORY OF MABS HOOPER

A heart home can be known so well
that feet are placed, weighted,
exactly in the eye's mind;

so well that blue
sings off a slope in every season
for its bluebells' song in May,

that flare of beech-branches
speaks always of rusted falls
and scratched, wrinkled leaf-piles,

never interrupts that long line of moor
louring from Meldon to Cawsand,
grasped as poetry, in need of no translation.

Thus the metre of your place, your life,
scanned like the carved pew-end
after years of touch in prayer,

rhymed like the running laughter of grandchildren.
This was the rhythm and stillness of your knowing –
speaking little, thinking and loving much,

and in that knowing
you in turn were known
and loved.

LUDLOW

Famous in my family history.
The last church my mother
ever tried to drag her squawling son around.
I am four. She is with *her* mother,

an elegant, disciplined lady of sixty-nine,
of the little-children-should-be-seen-but school.
We process around the church of Laurence the Martyr.
I make myself insufferable.

Fifty years on. In Ludlow by chance. Sight-line interrupted
by a high pillar, occluding the brightness
of a distant window. Long-dead connections
fire across the years. This was the place.

The church is very fine – it represents
all the best schools of English building.
It absorbs – as good churches do –
any amount of hopeless longing.

I do not regret my squawls.
I was four. But I would give them all –
and so much more – to talk with those two
as they were then, for half an hour

in that high space. About the Decorated porch,
and love, and discipline in growing old.
To feel the current of understanding between them,
which I remember, ever more faintly. I remember.

DARTMOOR - AFTER SNOW

A hard line of ground.
Once climbed, a land of mist -
oak woods conduct their winter chemistry,
sublime a white horizon-line
off purplish-brown branches.
The hill-tops respond, hiding their faces
in rolling, swaying smoke.
These are days that deride
my efforts at clarity, when sorrows
seem to laugh in my face.

Today, a day of deep snow thawing quickly,
a different sort of laughter scuffs the slopes
as snow-melt drifts sideways in waves,
mocking hill-mist and river-mist alike.
Today I still cannot lift your sadness
or find a formula to understand my own.
But out beyond Belstone
caught between these taxa of mist
I offer up a chill prayer of thanks
for this dance of unseeing.

VILLAGE FUNERALS

Fifteen years ago
I would have looked at myself
attending, *dulce et decorum*,
admired the grave style
with which I sat my pew,
and sang the sad hymns.

In fifteen more years
I'll be leaning
hard on the woodwork,
with the fixity of stare
my parents use
to look into death's approach.

So these are the good years,
when I grieve as much
for the old village, contemplating
depletion, as for myself, and call
my presence solidarity
rather than form, rather than anguish.

IV. The Ghost of Heraclitus

AXIS

The reader must pay attention.
If something is not immediately clear
Do not assume a mistake has been made.
My childhood au pair was called Jutte.
I remember her sunglasses and flaxen hair
And how I missed her when she left. Later
A harvest moon, the colour of blood, made all the difference.
Alcibiades sailed, against advice, for Sicily.
Chill-filtered flamingos rise out of a sea of bronze glass.
Alcibiades returns, and others are blamed.
We drive west, into a moonbow.
This larch wood, under the shadow of a hound,
Is a walled garden, and a lost friendship,
And love detained for years, without trial.
Do not assume a mistake has been made.
If something is not immediately clear
The reader must pay attention.

QUARTER TO FOUR

with thanks to Orhan Pamuk

The afternoon - perfect.
warm and bright for bluebell time.
Hammock precisely slung
allowing eyes an expanse of bluest sky.
But I am purposeful, this perfect afternoon.
I am reading a Turkish novel
about an ideal moment in a life -
The moment of the blue rose
precise apogee
of a man's happiness.
It comes on page seventy
leaving six hundred pages
for longing and regret.

It is quarter to four
on this hammock afternoon
at bluebell time.
I discover afterwards
from somewhere deep in the six hundred pages
that precisely at page seventy,
faint breeze toying with the new birch leaves,
a blackbird beginning to sing,
at the moment when I looked up to consider
ideal forms of blue
my watch stopped.
No matter.
Always I have a spare.

COUNSEL

Don't read that trash.
Even scientists should know Dante
Stretch into Eliot
Be able to discuss Ionesco.

Perhaps
Since I'm tied up at present
You should fall for someone else
Or join the Peace Corps.

Be careful.
That sort of touch
Is risky. Is like rocket fuel
With a celibate priest.

Two particles
Once twinned by interaction
Carry about always
A memory of the other's spin.

Remain silent
Among the ashes
For a week
Or as long as it takes.

THE POET AT HIS WINDOW

Clouds pedal across his territory
disguised as dragons
or the masks of wolves.

Their one intent
is to make themselves
into poems.

Their whole ambition
is to get past his bank-balance,
his pride, the mistakes he made with lovers.

In ever-shifting entreaty
the entire cosmos
presses itself against the glass

longing for him to see.

A CAFÉ IN NOTTING HILL

(where else?)
tourists ask me to take their picture.
I take six, digitise the father's calm latte,
the teenage daughter
fidgeting, striking dance poses
sitting abruptly on a curled leg
looking for herself.
                                        She is utterly found
in his love, even as he laughs at her,
and in the many poems that will be written
to that stern look, the grey eyes that stare the world down
longing to be noticed.
                                        Just be alive
I shout silently. Love the day with him,
the moment of becoming. Pay no attention
to the digitisers. Burn the Notting Hill poem.

THE COLOUR-CODED LIFE

I open a blue file at a pile of protocols, due for updating,
shut it hurriedly. That is tomorrow –
today I live in the green file, hector students,
recycle long-ago thoughts.
I live fluently in the green file, accept the need
to wake up to the blue.
It is a colour-coded life
in which I ration my surprises.
A student tells me she enjoyed talking,
but wonders at the violence of God.
A young poet has discovered Neruda – all this
is as it should be.
                                        It is not seeing a silver birch
as though all light, all greyness and birchness,
were in the luminosity of its bark.
It is not living
                                        as though the very act of living
were its own delight. Nor is it staring into a well
that opens suddenly in a long-familiar courtyard.

Once, my mother gave me a map. She had marked on it
where she would be in old age, so that I'd find her
and take her out for adventures. Once I saw an angel
in Japan. To leave you in that rainstorm was to drown
without remedy or calculation,
                                                                    to mean to say
we should meet again in love and freedom
                                                                                    and not say it.

Today, between files, I saw a swan stretch out its neck
and dive, plunge under the surface of a metal-dark river.
I saw it. Just for a moment.

FRAGMENT OF A 21ST-CENTURY *INFERNO*

Changing trains in a darkened wood
I am a burned-out camera;
I know what it is to die of desire.

Three beasts bar my way:
A leopard in Ray-Bans, an Al-Qaeda lion,
A genetically-modified she-wolf.

A train goes by for Eurodisney;
Another leaves for Srebrenica.
To wait here is itself to abandon hope.

A guide comes by – it is Bob Dylan at 70.

MY NEW FOUNTAIN PEN, MARKETED IN THREE LANGUAGES

English: The pleasure in writing

A BBC, if not a positively Civil Service
Reserve. On the instructions of the Minister
I have pleasure... Et cetera. Et cetera.

German: Die Lust am schreiben

The Germans know me so well.
There was desire there, and to its *Seduktiongeschichte* my credit
card succumbed.
A clear victory for Freud, and probably Schopenhauer.

French: L'irrésistible plaisir d'écrire

Ah, Paris, the prince of cities.
There they recognise with a commonsense shrug
That some lusts are irresistible. So much healthier.

THE MAN WHO IS NOT QUITE REAL

has no photographs of himself
except a tatty polaroid
with a long-idolised girl.

The man who is not quite real
has made an art-form
out of copying others.

He is a scientist, an artist,
a hillwalker, a student of Shakespeare,
depending who he last met, last lusted after.

He knows helium for a scarce resource,
roses for betrayal.
He knows exactly what he is supposed to like about jade.

He is into Raphael, Banksy, radical this or that.
He is waiting for someone to tell him
he is alive.

But he would not trust them if they did.
for no-one who comes to love him
can be quite real either.

They want to make a film now of an unreal life.
The man who is not quite real
watches, watches.

SHELVED WITH STEVENS AND SIDNEY

On some unspecified shelf
I sit near Wallace Stevens, tucked in
between him and the hero of Zutphen.
As flankers I claim
Rimbaud and Verlaine.

Shyly my work awaits its turn with the great,
to be moved from pile to pile,
shelf to bedside table,
string bag to shelf again,
to Oxfam and on.

I sediment in a rich silt,
carried along with amethysts and zircons,
the inner secrets of mystics,
outpourings of extroverts, geographies
of protest and heartbreak.

The van takes me away with the Dark Lady
and the Faerie Quene.
I migrate with the numinous doubt
of R.S.Thomas - sometimes,
by a category error, with Saki.

I shall be promoted at last,
without the option,
to some virtual Alexandria.
There my glory will be assured.

SELF-PORTRAIT OF THE ARTIST AS A BIRD OF PREY

He winds and winds himself up the sky
till he is an edge to a massing cloud
an iota on a hollow moon.

Yet he is printed with this valley,
these cliffs, he is never
long absent, this river

and its mists tag him,
the narrow stream
flows with his own life-blood.

Half his brain is seeing.
He is the contemplative
of this scudding sky

play-partner of its gales of wind.
From a great distance he catches sight
of a comma in the flux of the world,

stoops, strikes, searches,
feasts, looking constantly about him,
always alert to flee.

THE STATEMENT OF WANDERING AENGUS

I'll be out in January.
The section ends then, and they don't dare
try to renew it. Egg on their faces,
after the compensation claim.
Besides, there's a limit
even to Gung-Ho's power-trip.

We call him Gung-Ho
'cos he prescribes twice as many drugs
as the others, and keeps folk in
twice as long.
He's Dr Gunn-Hall to you.

I know where I'll go. I know exactly.
I'll go down to the little wood
where I last saw her. It was by
those stands of hazel. I'll start from there.
It was where they found me before,
in a thorn-bush. But that's where I have to start.

Yes, she's beautiful.
Yes I found her, and I have loved her always.
But it's not her loveliness I long for.
It's the light in her eyes and the sound
of my name on her lips.

I'll go down to the wood and start from there.
By that stand of hazel. In January.
I've got my old fishing-coat.
I'll start by the hazels
and walk down to that pool in the stream
where the trout rise.

Retrace your steps
my dad used to say
when you lose something.
My dad died, soon after they took me in.
Broke his heart, that last time.

I'll start by the hazels
at the first full moon of the year.
I'll take some fruit, in case I get peckish
while I'm looking.

CHANGE AT DUNDEE TAY BRIDGE

No man steps into the same river twice
– Heraclitus

For years the sky was high and light,
the river benign.
The air smelled of mountains.

I went south on these tracks
learning to savour
both hope and anxiety.

Once I saw you running to make the train
you thought I would be on
and took it for love.

On a long straight section of the bridge
leaving a family crisis
I saw a rainbow

and knew it
for the Lord's sign.

Another journey, later, and in a changed light.
The cantilevers, Victorian, stitch welded,
are no longer abstract exercises in stress

they are hatchings that hem my vision in.
And the curve, known from childhood, north to the city
no longer takes my eyes, my heart, on to family welcomes

but down, down, onto the stumps of the old bridge.
They jut from the lightless water,
supporting only the ghost of Heraclitus

I try to tell you
but we fall again to arguing;
neither of us can agree

what it was
the consultant said to us.

HAMMOCK WORK

You have to trust your hips
for the roll into the centre of the canvas
otherwise exit will be premature, and uncool.

You have to trust your eyes
to monitor the sway of high branches
to dissolve accurately in the immensity of sky.

Then you have to trust those hips again
to impart the slight rocking motion
not too fast, not too slow.

Crucially, you have to trust your eyes
to close at just the right moment
catching God in his heaven.

It's a bit like diving off a cliff,
this sort of work,
a lot of trust is involved.

THINGS TO PUT STRAIGHT AFTER MY DEATH

My requests are modest. Sign here
For the fame of these few small tasks.

4.2GB of mind-numbing protocols, called things like
Redress in respect of inadequate responses to non-vexatious
complaint.
For the love of God, delete them all.

Thirty box-files of notes in minute writing
What Pevsner said about mannerism
What Crick said about Watson
My one original thought on Dante. Discard, with regret.

My postmodern masterpiece, set in Obamaland
Sometime at the end of history, and still in note form.
Miglior-fabbricate it, I pray,
So even my savagest critics concede
'This was worth the Nobel, had he lived.'

Those old love-letters, in a vodka box,
(which, in truth, I lost years ago
And only occasionally lament).
Assemble the authors at the ages they were then.
Kiss them, long and tenderly,
And publish their effusions verbatim.

The air around my desk on my best day,
The shudder in the clock as it prepares to strike.
The long calm of the oaks in Front Meadow.
My cat's certain knowledge
That she is
The black cat at the centre of the universe.
Preserve holographically my joy in these things.

As you see, my demands are modest. Just sign here.

V. The Eighth Day

RENDERING VOICES

a poem for the 400th anniversary of the King James Bible

To begin on the Bible
To be caught by the rise of a huge wave breaking
To know all the conflict and chaos to be faced
If their book could not command
The nation, the language, in a foment of becoming.
They heard Scripture's ancient voices, remote,
Tasting of the desert,
Its longing, in a strange land.

Their task they called
A paradise of trees of life. Long hard years
They walked in this forest,
Dividing it into six sections,
Into exercise books, trading
Sigla and suggestions in rooms
Where kings had died and disciplines
Had been invented.

They threw strained eyes up at ceilings
Of hammer-beams, at gilt stars.
Every section was read aloud, the company
Some with eyes closed, some stroking pomaded beards,
Listening like poets at a workshop
For a false footfall, for any hint
Of ugliness. Only the words that formed
Like birds in the mouth, only they survived.

The ancient voices still arrive out of the past
Like a time capsule. They are smuggled
Into harsh places. They are raked over
On revisionist laptops. We bring to them

Immense science, but less confidence
That our words, put to the anvil, rubbed and polished
By the right number of learned men
Will last, or that they should.

Still the wave breaks over us
Shifting us in our chaos
Still it makes, in every age and tongue,
Insistent claims

In the beginning God
                                        The Lord is my shepherd
Vanity of vanities
                                        We beheld his glory
The glory as of the only begotten of the Father
Full of grace and truth.

My copy, given to me at three months old, is inscribed
In my godmother's hand. I treasure it. In student essays
I insist on the NRSV.
I download parables from *The Message*,
                                                                preach on them,
But it is the words that survived the tyrannous scrutiny
Of the beard-stroking poets, the birds in the mouth,
The words given me as a young child
That I will hear in my head when I am dying.

***

Commissioned by the Nida Institute for Biblical Scholarship at the American Bible Society, in collaboration with the Society of Biblical Literature, for presentation at the International Meeting of the Society of Biblical Literature at King's College London, July 2011.

Dedicated to my godmother Barbara William-Olsson (1921-2010), who gave me my first copy of the King James Bible. Love suffers long, and is kind.

THE GENESIS OF SIN

from 'Adam und Eva' by Max Beckmann

Simply this:
Eve with a cynical curl of the lips
Holds a pendulous breast
Cupping it into the shape of a peach.

(Even the gizzard-gazed dog-serpent
Wound tightly round the tree
For his own protection
Is visibly shocked.)

She is every whore in history
And Adam every honest burgher
Who puts up a shunning hand
And stares out from behind it
One eye naïve, the other cruel, actuarial.

THIS ALSO IS NOT THOU

Cadence

A star
becomes a star
becomes a leaf
eaten by a worm
which becomes a being
who can cast eyes heavenward
and say
there is no God.

Communiqué

I am not this or that
Rather I am pure other.

I do not desire the blood of bulls
I weep no tears over all that pap.

Purity of heart interests me

When there is darkness over the land
You see and do not see me.

EXILE

In Babylon, everything came clear
Sitting by the fountains and ziggurats,
Tending the gardens of the oppressor
Nights crammed into garrets
Or harems. Watching the foreigners' pomp,
Its meticulous infrastructure,
They understood their sin, the slump
In their vision. They had traded their future
For surfaces, slaked their need for prayer
With style and footballers' wives.
In the gardens they saw the desert's glory –
They saw the rigour of lives
Stretched out at the feet of the Lord.
They heard the Babylon-encompassing hugeness of his song,
Hard, cosmic, brooding, and they sang.

INTERVIEW WITH NICODEMUS

There are a good many signs and wonders
these days. I have not gone in
for that sort of thing very much.
There are others who delight in deciphering
the tricks of magicians, and the protestations
of would-be deliverers.
It has been enough for me to know
God's Law, and teach it
and do the relevant committee work.

I begin with that statement –
it is important to set something down;
the record depends on it. We annotate
what God gave us long ago.

I thought he was a man who deserved
a fair hearing. By night, yes,
but not like a terrorist or a thief.
Simply a man prudent of his colleagues.

It went as badly, and as well
as I could possibly have imagined.
What is this theology we play at? A game
for children? I came away a child.

I can tell you exactly. I memorised it
though it kept slipping away as I hurried back
through streets elusive with shadow.
In the end I wrote it down
in Hebrew and Latin and Greek,
the three languages of significance to God,
and hid the tablet in an old well
in my garden.

If it is ever found I will be a martyr
or a hero, unsatisfactory roles for a teacher
of the Law. There is one phrase
that stays with me always.
It is the colour of the night in those streets
and the sound of my heart pumping;
it has about it a dangerous tang of joy, and
he spoke it as though he were the wind himself.

When I feel myself dying I will teach it
at the Gate of Beauty - Gamaliel,
if he is alive, will save me a lynching.
"The Spirit blows where it wills. You hear
the sound of it, but you do not know where
it comes from, or where it is going.
so with everyone who is born of spirit."

I digress. We have talked enough.
I have nothing to say.
I watch and I wait.

BAPTISTRIES

The hidden room in a Roman house
a sunken basin in stone
beside it a narrow bench
the seat of the bishop
who slips in and out
wary of the imperial police.

***

Grand scholastic octagons
one side for each day of creation
the eighth for risen life.
Dignitaries in procession –
above them, heavenward,
Christ mosaiced in glory.

***

A river through an arid land
deep enough to drown in
beyond it a seamless robe.
The sky watches
full of flung wings.
The water teaches.
Every drop glistens
on the body of the carpenter's son,
falls from him reluctantly.
The air waits
charged with hope
death in it.

THE CUP

I played my part.
I am heavy two-handled Roman silver.
I am used for wine, volcanic wine of Orvieto,
Apulian red. Rot-gut Palestinian stuff
all resins and tannins
when the Procurator's steward forgets.

I was filled with water that day
pumped up from the Gihon
through that old tunnel - some long-dead king's -
chill and clear
drawn from the life-blood of the city.
And the Procurator washed his hands.

My surface reflected his face,
narrowed eyes,
terse lips, frown.
He flung the beads of water
not at the prisoner
but at the waiting crowd.

Other things happened that day.
There was a thunderstorm towards evening
clearing the air, replenishing the aquifers.
It was cold again that night;
they lit the brazier again
in the courtyard.

Tears were cried into me that night.
Tears of pointless scruple - his wife's,
wept into a good sweet Samian.
I am a Roman cup
robust, two-handled,
made for stronger stuff than tears.

DARK RELIEF

I come on to kill the mood
if there's any jollity about
or even worse, hint of joy.

In my time I've blighted Chaplin and Cleese,
mocked Socrates and ridiculed the Buddha,
seen zits on the face of Helen of Troy.

I had trouble only with the Nazarene.
He had that gift that some – a few – have
of making others feel better about the world.

But in his case it lasted – they stayed changed –
his own shoulders slumped a fraction more each time
but the sodding woman at the well, and fucking Zacchaeus,

I've heard the stories
too many times.
They stayed changed.

I saw him towards the end
the weight of the cross on his back
seeming to fit somehow. Seeming to complete him.

There passed between us
I remember
a look of total understanding.

He took in my hatred of all delight.
He saw my inescapable calling
and I saw his.

I come on to kill the mood.
It's what I do.
But without savour,

without zest, pride in my work,
since that day
in ugly, fetid old Jerusalem
the mood too dark to kill.

A LATE EASTER

Magnolia blossom on leaving church. Bees
busy at the petals' scent.
Chenin, Muscadet, Traminer,
heady as first loving.

Reliable sunlight
plays round the edge of a single cloud at evening.
Apricot, tangerine, vermilion,
bright as your smile in a crowd.

An avenue of limes
on Good Friday
a green mosaic
sweet as new faith.

COMPLINE

Into thy hands
I commend my spirit.
It fits in them
Exactly.

THE WOODWORKER AND THE POET

for Bill Hooper

We stood before the Christmas crib, the church's
Proud acquisition - you I knew had made
The frame, had sanded, stained, jointed it -
And what, you asked, what does a poet do?
A maker, I said - knee-jerk answer,
Schoolboy Greek - a poet is a maker.

I wanted all the time to run my hand
Across the finely-finished wood - you watched me
Want that, your gift securely jointed to life:
Words are precarious, dishonoured,
Their making a high conceit for humans, as is
Affecting to see into the grain of things.

Think of the power of words, I said, to make
Great lies. Strip them out - shape them new -
That is the poet's chore. You smiled, and I,
Relieved to satisfy you, turned to the holy scene.
A chance, for once, at strong-jointed joy -
Your making, humble, full of honest doubt,

Houses the saving word.

IMPRESSIONS OF FAITH

'(my faith), which was never strong, is being beaten into mere gold leaf, and flutters in weak rags from the letter of its old forms'

– Ruskin, writing to Henry Acland

Icons crack, split. Gold
Peels from the Pantocrator,
Hangs in shining rags.

What the heart looked to
Is a flickering image
On a beaten surface.

Gold leaf, atoms thin,
Lacks all mechanical strength,
Focusses X-rays.

These three things remain:
A flutter of beaten gold,
Slender hope, fierce love.

CHAPLAIN'S SONNET

for K.H.

Speaking of God. Speaking without answers.
Stretching slippery words into the suicide
Of a girl for want of beta-blockers.
Postulating a rock in a bad tide
Racing to ebb.
                                        Shake the grieving hands.
Feel a solidarity that calls not
On the name of God, defiantly bands
Together, accepts its bitter lot.

Live out the God-job. Call clangingly
For access of joy, and feel on your face
Friends' scepticism, stingingly.
God-words, they say, have lost their place.
Whatever is true and good, they say, think you
On those things. Reach always for the true.

FOR ROMESH MOLLIGODA, SEVENTEEN DAYS OLD, WITH THANKFULNESS

I hold my great-nephew for the first time.
He weighs six pounds. He is wrinkly, and perfect,
and makes a series of faces at me.

I know nothing of babies.
Successions of frown, fury, serenity
cross the face of this sleeping prince, as he dreams in
his new world.

I hold him with a secret passion
willing him to breathe
every next breath.

I consider the disturbing thought that without performing,
or exceeding targets, or outshining others,
I was once held, and gave deep happiness
to aunts and great-uncles and others, unknown lovers,

old spirits of seething intensity, unrequited rage at all the rest
of this blinkered world, stopped and at peace
in moments of fearful, breath-held, breath-expectant,
undoubted joy.

GLYDER FAWR FROM CWM IDWAL

Still, pure, glaciated bowl.
In a blizzard a soft, huge-walled space,
Slabs silted white, whole
Rim hidden by the storm's race:
A stretching place.

Summer redefines, reveals the shape
Of crags around the lake. Gulls
Dispute a tiny island. Steep
Tracks, walker-ridden, erode to shales:
Isolation fails.

Twll Du, they call the waterfall.
Devil's Kitchen. A wet black overhang,
Light-hiding hall
Of chaotic noise. Climbers cling,
Savour danger's song.

Above is another, mistier microcosm.
Scree, above that a boulder-bed.
If Satan be allowed his hanging chasm
This higher, broken city of the dead
Must be the Lord's

For only God, and the jesting raven,
Fox, steady on jumbled bone,
Dark-cheeked dark-eyed intentness of peregrine,
Only they would live up here, alone
With so much doubt and stone.

RIVER

'On the Sabbath day we went out of the gate by the river, where we thought there would be a place of prayer' (Acts 16.13)

We found a bright pool
the light almost too hard to look at
and rested there for a while.

We found a quick place
where the driving water
made arrows of foam.

Later, a long slow brown slide
under great trees.
We saw ourselves sharp in reflection

until suddenly we were in a great torrent
a place of such buffeting
that our spirits were thrashed upside down, whirled sideways,

spat out from there, washing up
on an island of old stone
not knowing the place, but feeling somehow known,
all the time wondering.